Math *in a* Democracy

by Erin Ash Sullivan

Table of Contents

CHAPTER 1

What Is a Democracy?

What is a **democracy**? The word *democracy* comes from the Greek words *demos,* meaning "people," and *kratein,* meaning "rule." So democracy is rule by the people. The people may rule directly, by casting votes to make decisions. That's direct democracy. Or the people may rule indirectly, by choosing representatives to make decisions. That's representative democracy.

You see democracy in action in everyday life. At recess your classmates vote informally on whether to play handball or basketball. Your city votes formally on whether to ban smoking in public places. Every four years, eligible **citizens** in the United States vote for the president.

More than 2,500 years ago, citizens of Athens, Greece, had one of the earliest democratic governments. Many citizens had the right to speak and vote at the city's assembly.

At about the same time, the people of Rome also chose democracy. Each year Roman citizens elected two consuls, the top decision-makers in the government. Rome also had a senate. Some senators were chosen by the consuls, and some were elected by the citizens.

These ancient democracies did not represent all the people, however, because only male citizens had a vote. Women and slaves could not vote.

IT'S A FACT!

The Native Americans of the Northeast created the first democracy in North America. For many years, the Mohawk, Oneida, Onondaga, Cayuga, and Seneca fought bitterly. Then around 1570, a man named Hiawatha brought them together as the Iroquois League. A Great Council ruled the Iroquois League. It was made up of 10 men from each tribe, chosen by the women for their bravery and wisdom.

ople are free to display eir choices. These are mpaign buttons.

The History of U.S. Democracy

T he United States was a new country in 1787 In May of that year, the greatest men of the day—George Washington, Alexander Hamilton, James Madison, and others—gathered in Philadelphia, Pennsylvania, for the Constitutional Convention. Their goal was to write a **constitution**, or a plan for the country's government.

Over the next four months, the **delegates** discussed many questions. How should the government be organized? What responsibilities should each branch of the government have? How long should elected officials serve? How should each state be represented? The delegates argued late into the nights during that summer.

Then on September 17, 1787, the delegates signed the new Constitution. In order to make it the law of the land, two-thirds of the states—nine of them—had to **ratify**, or approve, it. By the following summer, 11 of the 13 states had ratified the Constitution.

Constitutional Convention Time Line

May 25, 1787	August 6, 1787	August 7, 1787	September 1
Constitutional Convention begins	Delegates complete a rough draft of the Constitution	Delegates discuss who will be eligible to vote	Delegates s final draft of Constitutio convention

General George Washington presided over the Constitutional Convention, which convened in Philadelphia, Pennsylvania.

At the same time, James Madison wrote the Bill of Rights. These 10 **amendments** to the Constitution protect individual rights, such as freedom of speech and freedom of worship.

Solve This!

1. Use the time line of the Constitutional Convention to answer the following questions.

   a. Exactly how many days did the Constitutional Convention last?

   b. After Delaware ratified the Constitution, how many months passed before Rhode Island ratified it?

   c. How many years ago was the Constitution ratified?

December 7, 1787	June 21, 1788	May 29, 1790
Delaware is the first state to ratify the Constitution	The Constitution is ratified by the United States	Rhode Island is the last state to ratify the Constitution

The Three Branches of Government

The United States today is very different from the United States of 1787. However, the way our **federal** government, or the government of the whole country, works is basically the same. The authors of the Constitution designed a system that has survived more than two centuries of growth and change.

The federal government has three branches, or parts: the legislative, the executive, and the judicial. Each branch has its own powers and responsibilities. This is called the **separation of powers**. Each branch can check the decisions of the others. With power divided among three branches, no one branch becomes too powerful. This arrangement is called the system of **checks and balances**.

U.S. GOVERNMENT SYSTEM

The Branches of the U.S. Government

LEGISLATIVE BRANCH	EXECUTIVE BRANCH	JUDICIAL BRANCH
Senate, House of Representatives	President, vice president, departments	Supreme Court, federal court system

The Legislative Branch

At the federal level, the legislative branch is called Congress. Its job is to make laws. The laws may involve declaring war, creating taxes, and borrowing money.

Congress is made up of two separate but equal lawmaking groups, the Senate and the House of Representatives. Both the Senate and House must pass a **bill**—a proposed law—in order for it to become law. Then the president must sign it. If the president **vetoes** the bill, which means the president rejects it, or does not sign it, Congress can still make it law. It does so by having two-thirds of the members vote for it. This overrides the president's veto.

IT'S A FACT!

Delegates at the Constitutional Convention had a hard time deciding how to set up Congress. Larger states wanted representation to be based on population, whereas smaller states wanted each state to have the same number of representatives. Roger Sherman of Connecticut proposed the Great Compromise: Why not do both? That's just what they did. In the Senate, each state has two senators. In the House, the number of representatives depends on a state's population.

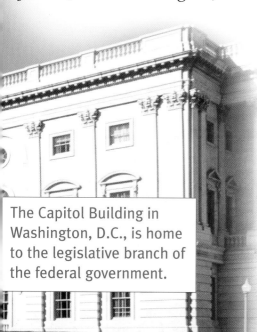

The Capitol Building in Washington, D.C., is home to the legislative branch of the federal government.

The Senate is one half of Congress. Each state elects two senators. A senator serves a six-year term. In order to become a senator, a person must be at least 30 years old, a resident of his or her state, and have been a U.S. citizen for at least nine years.

The Senate has specific responsibilities. Among them are approving any treaties the president makes with foreign countries and confirming those people the president chooses for high-level jobs.

The House of Representatives is the other half of the legislature. There are 435 representatives. The number of representatives per state depends on the state's population. States with larger populations have more representatives. A state with a very small population may have only one representative.

A representative must be at least 25 years old, a resident of his or her state, and a U.S. citizen for at least seven years.

The responsibilities of the House include introducing bills that call for new taxes or establish new national holidays.

Solve This!

2. Try some legislative math:

a. What is the minimum number of votes in the House needed to make up a majority? In the Senate?

b. How many votes does the House need for a two-thirds majority? How many does the Senate need?

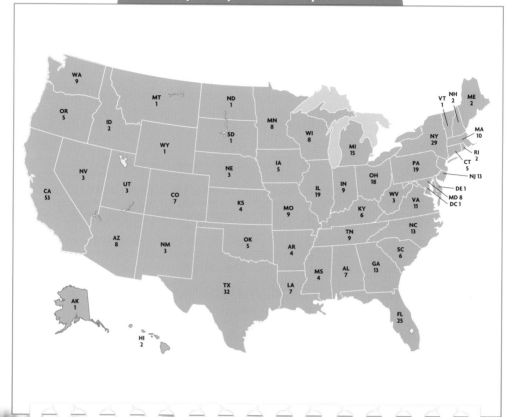

Map of Representatives per State

And This!

3. Use the map to answer these questions.

   a. How many more representatives does New York have than Florida?

   b. How many states have more representatives than Pennsylvania?

   c. What is the average number of representatives for Michigan, Illinois, Wisconsin, and Ohio?

   d. Find the six states that have the greatest number of representatives. Create a bar graph to present this data.

The Executive Branch

The executive branch of the government makes sure that the laws of the land are carried out. The president, the vice president, the 15 departments of the executive branch, and independent agencies make up the executive branch.

In order to become president, a person must be at least 35 years old and have lived in the United States for at least 14 years. He or she must have been born a U.S. citizen. Presidents serve terms of four years, and they may not serve more than two terms.

The president is the head of the armed forces. The president also makes treaties with foreign countries and chooses people to serve in top-level jobs, such as ambassadors and Supreme Court justices. The president also has the power to veto laws that Congress passes.

The president's group of advisers is called the cabinet. Each of the 15 cabinet members, or secretaries, heads a department. Each department focuses on a specific issue, such as education, the environment, the economy, and foreign relations.

On January 20, 2001, George W. Bush took the oath of office as the 43rd president of the United States with his wife and daughters looking on.

IT'S A FACT!

There are 15 specific departments that make up the executive branch. Their heads, or secretaries, sit as cabinet members. The cabinet is solely advisory to the president. In 2002, President George Bush created the Department of Homeland Security.

DEPARTMENTS

Department of Agriculture

Department of Commerce

Department of Defense

Department of Education

Department of Energy

Department of Health and
Human Services

Department of Homeland
Security

Department of Housing and
Urban Development

Department of Interior

Department of Justice

Department of Labor

Department of State

Department of Transportation

Department of Treasury

The Judicial Branch

The job of the judicial branch is to make sure that laws are constitutional and are interpreted and applied correctly. The judicial branch is made up of federal judges. It is headed by the Supreme Court, the most important court in the country.

There are nine justices on the Supreme Court. One is the Chief Justice. Justices are chosen by the president and approved by the Senate. A Supreme Court justice holds the position for life or until he or she wishes to retire.

Ruth Bader Ginsburg

David Hackett Souter

Clarence Thomas

Antonin Scalia

John Paul Stevens

Chief Justice William Hubbs Rehnquist

Part of the Supreme Court's job is to decide whether the country's laws are constitutional. This decision process is called **judicial review**. Sometimes the Supreme Court decides that a law is unconstitutional, or not in line with the rules set down by the Constitution. Then the law is overturned, or thrown out.

Solve This!

4. Use the data from the chart to answer these questions about today's justices of the Supreme Court.

a. What is the average age of the justices?

b. What is the range in age of the justices?

c. Which justice has been on the Supreme Court for the longest time? How long?

d. Which justice has been on the Supreme Court for the shortest time? How long?

Stephen Breyer

Sandra Day O'Connor

Anthony M. Kennedy

Supreme Court Justices		
Justice	Year Born	Year Appointed
Rehnquist	1924	1972
Stevens	1920	1975
O'Connor	1930	1981
Scalia	1936	1986
Kennedy	1936	1988
Souter	1939	1990
Thomas	1948	1991
Ginsburg	1933	1993
Breyer	1938	1994

Elections: The People Speak

Suffrage means "the right to vote." The United States Constitution gives suffrage to all eligible citizens. However, the definition of an eligible citizen has changed over the years.

In the first presidential election, in 1789, only six percent of all Americans were allowed to vote. Voting was limited to wealthy white men who owned property. The authors of the Constitution believed that only these people would be educated well enough to vote wisely.

In the 1820s, some states began changing the rules. Voters didn't have to own property anymore—but they still had to be white males.

 IT'S A FACT!

When Andrew Jackson was elected in 1828, he was so popular that he became known as the "People's President." Thousands of citizens came to Washington, D.C., to celebrate his inauguration, and many visited the

White House. Unfortunately, the crowds became so unruly that many of the White House furnishings were trampled and ruined.

Votes for African Americans

African-American men won the right to vote when Congress passed the Fifteenth Amendment in 1870. For about 20 years, some African Americans voted and were elected to public office.

However, in the 1890s, southern states took African Americans' voting rights away. States charged a poll tax, a fee for voting, that many could not afford. States also required literacy tests that many could not pass. In the 1960s, things began to change. Dr. Martin Luther King, Jr. and others led protests and marches to demand civil rights, such as the right to vote, for African Americans. Congress eventually passed laws that outlawed the poll tax and protected African Americans' voting rights.

Citizens marched on Washington, D.C., to demand civil rights on August 28, 1963.

Votes for Women

U.S. women began their fight for suffrage a long time ago. In 1848, Lucretia Mott and Elizabeth Cady Stanton led a meeting in Seneca Falls, New York, to discuss ways to get suffrage for women. They met strong resistance. Most men believed that women could not and should not vote.

For the next 70 years, thousands of women fought for suffrage. In 1919, Congress passed the Nineteenth Amendment, giving women the right to vote. The states ratified it in 1920. Women finally had the right to make their voices heard at the ballot box.

Solve This!

5. Answer the following questions.

   a. How many years passed between the meeting in Seneca Falls and the passage of the Nineteenth Amendment?

   b. In what year would the youngest voter in 1970 have been born?

   c. In what year would the youngest voter today have been born?

Women who believed in suffrage, called suffragists, marched to demand the right to vote. One of the most famous suffragists was Susan B. Anthony.

Voting Today

In order to vote today, a person must be 18 years old, a U.S. citizen, and a resident of the city and state where he or she votes. Citizens lose their right to vote if they have been convicted of a serious crime.

Until 1971, the minimum voting age was 21. The age was lowered because many of the soldiers who fought and died in the Vietnam War were as young as 18. Many people believed that those who were old enough to fight for their country should be allowed to vote. The Twenty-sixth Amendment changed the voting age to 18.

The Reverend Jesse Jackson ran for president in 1984 and 1988.

17

First-time voters have to **register**, or sign up. It's easy to do. In many states, people can register to vote at libraries and schools. In order to register, citizens must prove that they are residents of the cities, towns, boroughs, townships, and villages where they plan to vote.

When people register, they can also join a political party. A political party is a group of people who share beliefs about the role the government should play in citizens' lives. Political parties generally work to elect officials who will try to pass laws that the political party supports.

Solve This!

6. **The Republicans and Democrats haven't always been the nation's leading political parties. Look at this graph and answer the questions below.**

    a. **Which party has been around longest? For how long?**

    b. **Which party lasted longer, the Federalists or the Whigs? How much longer?**

    c. **How many years after the start of the Democratic party did the Republican party begin?**

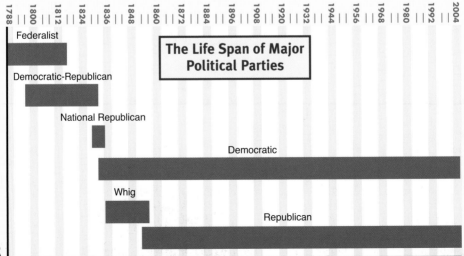

The Life Span of Major Political Parties

Federalist

Democratic-Republican

National Republican

Democratic

Whig

Republican

1788 1800 1812 1824 1836 1848 1860 1872 1884 1896 1908 1920 1932 1944 1956 1968 1980 1992 2004

The two main political parties in the United States today are the Republicans and the Democrats. In general, Republicans support the idea that government should not play a large part in individuals' lives. Democrats usually look to government to provide programs that help its citizens.

Someone who registers as a Democrat or a Republican is able to vote in **primaries**. Primaries are special elections each party holds in order to choose one **candidate** for each office in the main election. People who do not wish to register with one of the political parties can choose to be "Independent."

A convention to nominate, or choose, the candidates for president and vice president is held by each major political party.

Imagine that you're 18 and that it's election day. You're registered, you've read about the issues, and you've learned about the candidates. Now you're off to your polling place.

A **polling place** is a local voting site, such as a school or town hall. Each registered voter is assigned to vote at a specific polling place.

 Point

Think It Over

In the eighteenth century, voters announced their choices to the crowd at the polling place. Today people vote by secret ballot. What makes a secret ballot better? What problem could come from announcing your vote to the public?

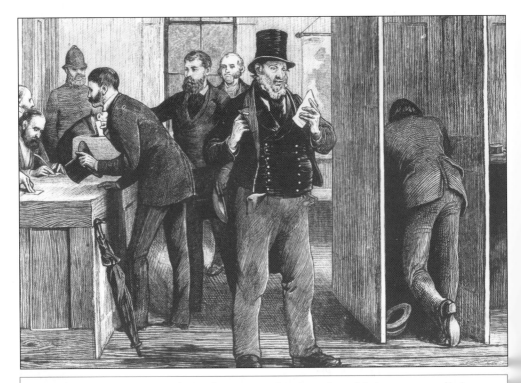

This illustration represents the 1873 election, in which men are lining up to receive their ballot papers. Notice the absence of women and African Americans.

After checking in with the poll workers and signing the voter book, you head to the voting booth. There you will cast your **ballot**, or the record of your votes.

All states use voting machines. With some voting machines, you cast your votes by flipping a series of small levers. The machine records your votes when you pull a large lever upon leaving the booth. Other booths use a computerized voting system; you touch a screen to make your ballot choices.

Solve This!

7. Some voters punch cards to vote. A computer reads the cards.

   a. At 1,000 cards per minute, how many cards can a computer read in one hour? Two hours?

   b. About how long would it take for a computer to read 100,000 cards? 500,000 cards?

High-tech touch-screen voting may become common in the future.

Paying for a Democracy

Our federal government needs money in order to run. Much of this money comes from the citizens in the form of taxes.

Everyone in the United States is familiar with taxes in one form or another. Property owners pay a tax based on the size and value of their property. Consumers pay a sales tax on items they buy. Buyers of items such as gasoline, cigarettes, and alcohol pay an additional tax.

Income Tax

The federal government's most important source of money is a tax on income. Most working people pay an income tax.

Do you know what the sales tax is in your state?

Solve This!

8. How much would you pay for a CD that costs $14.99 in Massachusetts? In New York? In California? In Texas?

State Sales Tax in Selected States	
California	6.00%
Massachusetts	5.00%
California	4.00%
Texas	6.25%

The income tax is equal to a percentage of the money they earn. For the most part, people who make more money pay a higher percentage of income tax than those who make less money.

Before 1913, there was no income tax. Workers kept all the money they made. Things changed when Congress passed the Sixteenth Amendment, which set up the Internal Revenue Service (IRS) to collect taxes. Tax laws have changed over the years.

Solve This!

9. Imagine that you earn $46,200 each year.

   a. How much do you earn monthly?

   b. The federal government takes 18 percent of your pay for income tax. How much do you pay annually in income tax?

U.S. tax laws are famous for being complicated and difficult to understand!

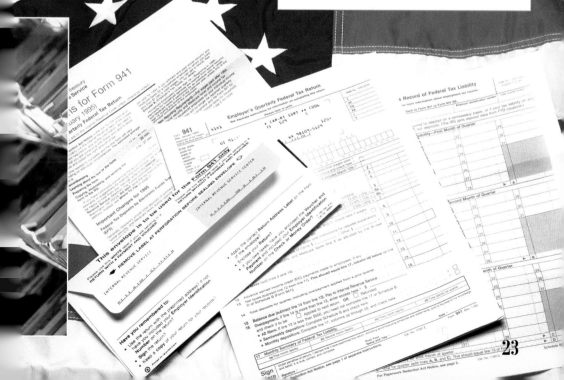

1999
Federal Budget Deficit

$ 0 !

The president outlines his goals every year before presenting the budget to Congress. The 1999 budget deficit as presented by President Bill Clinton and Vice President Al Gore was an amazing $0!

Preparing the Budget

How does the government decide what to spend? Each year the President creates a **budget**, a plan for spending, for the entire country. First the president and his advisers estimate how much money will be available to spend. Then each department prepares its own budget, asking for enough money to run its programs.

The president must balance the needs and wishes of each department with the money that is available. Usually, each department ends up revising its budget. Finally, the president gives the proposed budget to Congress, which must discuss and approve every item. Congress can add and subtract items as well.

The House of Representatives has the job of setting any new taxes—or tax cuts—in motion. It does this by writing bills. Then House and Senate committees work on the bills. Congress and the president must approve any changes that committees recommend.

Although government needs money in order to run, most people don't enjoy paying taxes. Most people get upset when their taxes increase. For this reason, elected officials are often unwilling to pass new tax laws. They don't want to be blamed for increasing taxes.

✔ Point

Talk About It

April 15 is tax-filing day. Cartoonists have lots of fun depicting the public's feelings about this annual event. What do you think the cartoonist is trying to say?

Solve This!

10. Suppose that you get an allowance of $15.00 each week. Create a budget for yourself. If you had to spend $1.00 on lunch each day, how would your budget change?

the arts

the environment

education

foreign aid

defense

health care

Services

Where does all the money from taxes go? These are just a few things the federal government pays for each year:

- Defense: maintaining the armed forces and developing defense technology
- Social services: providing help to elderly people through such programs as Social Security and Medicare and to needy families through Medicaid
- Education: helping local communities build schools, pay teachers, buy supplies
- Environment: preserving open spaces and maintaining parklands
- The arts: funding arts programs
- Foreign aid: helping countries in need.

The goal of any budget is to spend no more money than is available. Some budgets even try to spend less than what is available, so that the extra money—the **surplus**—can go into savings.

A government budget surplus is rare, however. More often the government spends more money than it actually has. This creates a budget **deficit.** The government gets the rest of the money it needs by taking out loans. One way for the government to borrow money is to sell bonds to its citizens.

Solve This!

11. Suppose that you paid $100 in taxes in 2002.
   a. How much of your money would be spent on defense, assuming it accounts for 16% of the budget?
   b. On education, assuming it accounts for 23% of the budget?
   c. On the environment, assuming it accounts for 12% of the budget?

This clock shows how much the government owes.

OUR NATIONAL DEBT:

OUR *Family share* $

THE NATIONAL DEBT CLOCK

ONAL DEBT INCREASE PER SECOND $ 10,000

1992 INTEREST COST – $292 BILLION

CHAPTER 5

A Healthy Democracy

The challenge for the United States in the future will be to keep its democracy strong and healthy. One key is to make sure that citizens continue to have fair voting opportunities. Another key is to make sure that citizens stay well informed about the issues.

For any democracy to remain strong and healthy, people must continue to make their voices heard. Despite increased voting opportunities, relatively fewer people come out to vote each year. In 1860, 81 percent of all registered voters voted in the presidential election. By 2000 that number dropped to about 52 percent.

Solve

12. **Find out what percentage of the voting-age population voted in each of these elections. What trend do you observe? Use a calculator if you wish.**

National Voter Turnout in Federal Elections: selected years 1960–2000				
Year	Voting Age Population	Registered	Turnout	Percentage of VAP
2000	205,815,000	156,421,311	105,586,274	
1992	189,529,000	133,821,178	104,405,155	
1984	174,466,000	124,150,614	92,652,680	
1976	152,309,190	105,037,986	81,555,789	
1968	120,328,186	81,658,180	73,211,875	
1960	109,159,000	64,833,096	68,838,204	

VAP=Voting Age Population

Why do so many people choose not to vote? Some find it difficult to take the time to vote. Others find it hard to learn about the issues. Many think that their votes don't matter. However, in a democracy every vote matters.

Even if you're not yet old enough to vote, you can still be part of a democracy. You can participate at the local and state levels. You can learn more about the issues that are important to you. You can write letters to your senators and representatives. You can talk to older people who can vote. You can urge them to register and vote, and you can tell them where you stand on the issues.

You can be a part of the democratic process by stating your views and supporting student government.

Solve This!

1. page 5:
   a. 116 days;
   b. 29 months;
   c. 215 years (in 2003)
2. page 8:
   a. House needs 218 for a majority and Senate needs 51; House needs 290 for a two-thirds majority and Senate needs 67.
3. page 9:
   a. 4; b. 4; c. 15;

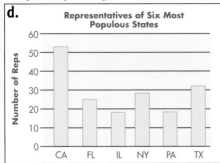

d.
   Representatives of Six Most Populous States

4. page 13:
   a. 68 years (in 2003);
   b. 28 years;
   c. Rehnquist, 31 years (in 2003);
   d. Breyer, 9 years (in 2003)
5. page 16:
   a. 71 years;
   b. 1949; c. 1985 (in 2003)
6. page 18:
   a. Democratic Party, 171 years (in 2003); b. Federalists, 8 years;
   c. 20 years

7. page 21:
   a. 60,000 cards; 120,000 cards;
   b. 100 minutes, or one hour and 40 minutes; 500 minutes, or eight hours and 20 minutes
8. page 22:
   $15.74; $15.59; $15.89; $15.93
9. page 23:
   a. $3,850; b. $8,316
10. page 25:
   Answers will vary; with $1.00 for lunch each day, discretionary income drops to $8.00 each week.
11. page 27:
   a. $16.00; b. $23.00;
   c. $12.00
12. page 28

Year	Percentage of VAP
2000	51.3%
1992	55.1%
1984	53.1%
1976	53.5%
1968	60.8%
1960	63.1%

Glossary

amendment   (uh-MEND-ment) a law added to the Constitution (page 5)

ballot   (BAL-luht) a record of a voter's votes, sometimes on a slip of paper (page 21)

bill   (BIHL) a proposed law (page 7)

budget   (BUJ-eht) a plan for spending money (page 24)

candidate   (KAN-dih-dayt) someone who is running for office (page 19)

checks and balances   (CHEHKS and BAL-uhn-suhz) each branch of the government can check the decisions of the others (page 6)

citizen   (SIH-tih-sen) someone who lives in a country and shows loyalty to it (page 2)

constitution   (kon-sti-TOO-shuhn) a plan for a government (page 4)

deficit   (DE-fuh-sut) in a budget, the amount by which expenses exceed income (page 27)

delegate   (DEL-eh-geht) a representative at a meeting (page 4)

democracy   (duh-MAHK-ruh-see) a system of government in which the citizens make decisions by voting (page 2)

federal   (FED-er-uhl) at the national level (page 6)

judicial review   (joo-DISH-uhl ree-VYOO) the process by which the Supreme Court decides whether the country's laws are constitutional (page 13)

polling place   (POHL-ing PLAYS) a local voting site (page 20)

primary   (PRIGH-mair-ee) a special election held by political parties to choose candidates for general elections (page 19)

ratify   (RAT-ih-figh) to approve a law (page 4)

register   (REJ-ih-ster) to sign up to vote (page 18)

separation of powers   (sehp-uh-RAY-shun uv POW-erz) each branch of the government has its own powers and responsibilities (page 6)

suffrage   (SUHF-rehj) the right to vote (page 14)

surplus   (SER-pluhs) in a budget, the amount by which income exceeds expenses (page 27)

veto   (VEE-toh) to say no to (page 7)

Index